BRIGHTEN YOUR SMILE

and Other Amazing Advice

Betsy Rossen Elliot

Contents

Home Remedies and Beauty Tips

Visit a drugstore or the personal care department of most grocery stores, and you'll be amazed at the number, variety, and cost of products available to keep you neat, clean, and healthy. Even more amazing is that the same work can be done by baking soda—solo or teamed up with other everyday products—more effectively and less expensively. Plus, good ol' bicarbonate of soda is strong yet safe for your whole family. No wonder that reassuring ARM & HAMMER logo has been around so long!

TEETH AND TOOTH TOOLS

◆ To make your own toothpaste, mix 4 teaspoons ARM & HAMMER Baking Soda with 1 teaspoon Morton Salt. Add a small spoonful of glycerin and mix until it is the right consistency for toothpaste. Add a few drops of McCormick Pure Peppermint, Pure Mint, Pure Anise, or Cinnamon Extract to taste. Spoon into a small, airtight squeeze bottle.

◆ Use ARM & HAMMER Baking Soda as toothpaste—or add a little to your child's regular toothpaste—to help remove plaque buildup.

◆ Soak dentures, athletic mouthguards, retainers, or other oral appliances in a solution of 2 teaspoons ARM &

HAMMER Baking Soda dissolved in a glass of warm water. Another option is to scrub these items with a Reach toothbrush dipped in baking soda.

FRESHEN UP

◆ Remove fish, onion, or garlic odor from hands with a solution of 3 parts ARM & HAMMER Baking Soda to 1 part water or Ivory Liquid Hand Cleanser. Rub, then rinse.

◆ To freshen breath, use 1 teaspoon ARM & HAMMER Baking Soda in half a glass of water; swish the solution through your teeth, then rinse.

◆ For a simple daily deodorant, dust ARM & HAMMER Baking Soda under arms using a powder puff.

Bubbly Beginnings

In 1846, New Englanders John Dwight and his brother-in-law, Dr. Austin Church, became the first U.S. commercial manufacturers of bicarbonate of soda. They took trona, or soda ash, out of the ground and turned it into what's commonly called baking soda. The company was eventually called Church & Dwight Co., Inc.

James A. Church, the son of Dr. Church, joined the company in 1867 and brought his ARM & HAMMER trademark from his own Vulcan Spice Mills (named after the Roman god of fire, skilled at forging armor). The ARM & HAMMER symbol was applied to some Church & Dwight baking soda packages; it soon became the most popular and then primary brand. The ARM & HAMMER symbol became part of the Church & Dwight logo as well.

- Freshen up with a washcloth dipped in a solution of 4 tablespoons ARM & HAMMER Baking Soda and 1 quart water.

HANDNOTES AND FOOTNOTES

- If your hands are freshly stained with water-based paint, wash and scrub them with ARM & HAMMER Baking Soda. Dig your fingernails right into the soda to clean them too.

- Smooth rough and hardened calluses and heels by massaging with a paste of 3 parts ARM & HAMMER Baking Soda to 1 part water.

- Soak tired feet in a basin of warm water with 3 tablespoons ARM & HAMMER Baking Soda.

THE FACE SPACE

- Mix ARM & HAMMER Baking Soda with Old Fashioned Quaker Oats in your blender; it makes a great facial scrub.

- Make a paste of 3 parts ARM & HAMMER Baking Soda to 1 part water and use as a gentle, exfoliating facial scrub after washing with soap and water. Rinse clean.

- For instant relief of razor burn, dab on a solution of 4 tablespoons ARM & HAMMER Baking Soda to 1 quart water.

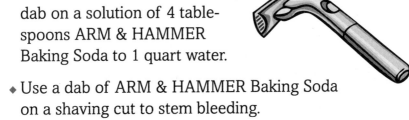

- Use a dab of ARM & HAMMER Baking Soda on a shaving cut to stem bleeding.

BODY LANGUAGE

- Make bubbling bath salts with 2½ cups ARM & HAMMER Baking Soda, 2 cups McCormick Cream of Tartar, and ½ cup Argo Corn Starch. Mix ingredients together and store in a covered container. Use ¼ cup per bath.

- Relieve itchy skin during the winter by pouring 1 cup ARM & HAMMER Baking Soda and 1¼ cups Johnson's Baby Oil into your bath.

- Rub a paste of ARM & HAMMER Baking Soda and water onto elbows to smooth away rough skin.

CARE FOR YOUR HAIR

- Add a teaspoon of ARM & HAMMER Baking Soda to a bottle of your usual shampoo to help remove buildup from conditioner, mousse, and hairspray, as well as to improve manageability.

- Rinse hair with ½ teaspoon ARM & HAMMER Baking Soda in 1 pint water to remove the dullness or discoloration caused by chlorinated pools.

- In a pinch, use ARM & HAMMER Baking

Well, Naturally

Baking soda is a naturally occurring, very versatile substance that's environmentally safe and inexpensive. Not only is baking soda nontoxic, it is actually a food—so unlike many commercial household products, it is safe to use around children and pets.

Soda as a dry shampoo for oily hair. Sprinkle on and comb through, then fluff hair with a blow-dryer.

BURNS AND BITES

◆ For sunburn pain, saturate a washcloth with a solution of 4 tablespoons ARM & HAMMER Baking Soda in 1 quart water. Apply to affected area.

◆ Make a soothing paste for a bug bite or sting by combining equal parts Morton Salt and ARM & HAMMER Baking Soda, then mixing with a little water. Apply to the affected area with a Rite Aid cotton ball.

TUMMY RUMBLES

◆ Take ½ teaspoon ARM & HAMMER Baking Soda in half a glass of water to relieve acid indigestion or heartburn. Read antacid use information on the ARM & HAMMER Baking Soda package before using. *Warning: People who must restrict salt intake should not use ARM & HAMMER Baking Soda as an antacid. Do not take for nausea, stomachaches, gas, cramps, or distension from overeating.*

◆ Try this elixir as a remedy for nausea: Mix 1 cup water, 10 drops ReaLime Lime Juice, and ½ teaspoon Domino Sugar. Add ¼ teaspoon ARM & HAMMER Baking Soda. Drink.

Housecleaning

Can the mild-mannered crystals known as baking soda really clean? Yes! Baking soda has been doing a number on dirt and grime for generations. Whether on its own offensive mission or boosting the power of other cleaners, ARM & HAMMER Baking Soda is on your side, from carpets to windows to kitchen appliances to bathrooms and back again. The forces of yuck have met their match...and then some.

WINDOWS, WALLS & WOOD

◆ Put dirty venetian blinds in a tub of warm water; add ½ cup ARM & HAMMER Baking Soda, soak for half an hour, then scrub and rinse.

◆ For cleaning walls or other painted surfaces: Combine 1 cup Parsons' Ammonia, 1 cup ARM & HAMMER

All-Purpose Cleanser

This homemade concoction can replace most of the commercial cleansers you probably have on your shelf.

1 teaspoon 20 Mule Team Borax
1 teaspoon ARM & HAMMER Baking Soda
2 teaspoons Heinz Distilled White Vinegar or ReaLemon Lemon Juice
¼ teaspoon Dawn dishwashing liquid
2 cups hot water

Be sure to wear rubber gloves when working with this mixture. Mix and store in a clearly labeled spray bottle.

Baking Soda, and 1 gallon water. Apply mixture with an O-Cel-O sponge, scrubbing marks gently. No need to rinse. Wear gloves to protect your hands from the ammonia.

◆ Remove crayon marks from walls with a damp O-Cel-O sponge dipped in ARM & HAMMER Baking Soda.

◆ Rub out white rings on wood tables with a paste made of equal parts Crest toothpaste and ARM & HAMMER Baking Soda.

KITCHEN PATROL

Countertops and Other Surfaces

◆ Use this homemade solution to cut grease buildup on stoves, backsplashes, tiles, and glossy enamel surfaces: Mix ¼ cup ARM & HAMMER Baking Soda, ½ cup Heinz Distilled White Vinegar, 1 cup Parsons' Ammonia, and 1 gallon hot water. Wear rubber gloves and use in a well-ventilated area.

◆ Remove stains on laminated countertops with a paste of ARM & HAMMER Baking Soda and water. Apply, let dry, then rub off and rinse.

◆ Stainless-steel sinks and other surfaces can be cleaned with a paste of ARM & HAMMER Baking Soda and water, or by sprinkling baking soda directly onto an O-Cel-O sponge and scrubbing the surface. Rinse and buff dry.

- Rub a wood cutting board with a paste of ARM & HAMMER Baking Soda and water to remove odors.

Appliances

- To clean sticky refrigerator door gaskets, mix 4 tablespoons ARM & HAMMER Baking Soda with 1 quart water; apply with a Reach toothbrush. Wipe clean. This also helps control mildew buildup.

- To remove any unpleasant taste in ice cubes from an automatic ice cube maker, clean the removable parts of the unit with ARM & HAMMER Baking Soda and water.

- Clean the inside and outside of a microwave with a little ARM & HAMMER Baking Soda on a damp O-Cel-O sponge; rinse well.

- For a thorough oven cleaning, leave an ovenproof dish containing 1 cup Parsons' Ammonia in a cold, closed oven overnight to loosen dirt. In the morning, wipe away ammonia from oven surfaces; sprinkle with ARM & HAMMER Baking Soda and then wipe clean with a damp O-Cel-O sponge.

Neat Kitchen Tips

- Baking soda and vinegar will foam your drain clean and help prevent clogs. Pour ½ cup ARM & HAMMER Baking Soda down the drain, followed by 1 cup Heinz Distilled White Vinegar. When foam subsides, rinse with hot water. This also works well on garbage disposals.

- Periodically wash out and deodorize garbage cans with a solution of 1 cup ARM & HAMMER Baking Soda per gallon of water.

THE BATHROOM BATTLE

- Try this basic bathroom cleaner for everyday cleaning. Mix together 3 tablespoons ARM & HAMMER Baking Soda, ½ cup Parsons' Ammonia, and 2 cups warm water. Or skip the ammonia and mix 1 box (16 ounces) ARM & HAMMER Baking Soda, 4 tablespoons Dawn dishwashing liquid, and 1 cup warm water. Mix well and store in a well-labeled spray or squeeze container. Be sure to wear rubber gloves and use in a well-ventilated area.

- A simple paste of ARM & HAMMER Baking Soda and water will attack hard-water or rust stains on ceramic tile. Use a nylon scrubber, then rinse.

Bathtubs and Showers

- Adding ARM & HAMMER Baking Soda to bathwater will reduce the ring around the tub and soften your skin. Use 2 tablespoons for a full tub of water.

- Remove mineral buildup and improve your showerhead's performance with this remedy: In a GLAD Food Storage Zipper Bag, mix ½ cup ARM & HAMMER Baking Soda and 1 cup Heinz Distilled White Vinegar. Secure the plastic bag around the showerhead with  a rubber band so the showerhead is submerged in the solution; let sit for 1 hour. Remove bag and run very hot water through showerhead for several minutes.

- For tough grout or tile stains, use a paste of 1 part Clorox Regular-Bleach to 3 parts ARM & HAMMER Baking Soda.

Toilets

- Remove stubborn stains in the toilet bowl by scrubbing with fine steel wool dipped in ARM & HAMMER Baking Soda.

- For a homemade toilet bowl cleaner, mix 1 cup ARM & HAMMER Baking Soda with 1 cup Tide powdered laundry detergent. Each time you clean, sprinkle ¼ cup of this mixture into the toilet and let it sit 10 minutes. Scrub briefly, then let it sit another 10 minutes. Brush again, then flush.

FLOORS, FURNITURE & FURNISHINGS

- Once a month, sprinkle carpets with ARM & HAMMER Baking Soda. Let sit overnight, then vacuum.

- To clean and deodorize baby spills or accidents on carpeting, first soak up as much of the mess as possible with a clean rag or Scott Towel. When dry, sprinkle with ARM & HAMMER Baking Soda; let sit 15 minutes before vacuuming.

- Remove water spots on wood floors with an O-Cel-O sponge dampened in a solution of 4 tablespoons ARM & HAMMER Baking Soda and 1 quart warm water.

- To erase a water ring from finished wood, mix a small quantity of ARM & HAMMER Baking Soda with Crest toothpaste. Apply the paste to the affected area with a clean, soft cloth; gently rub. Wipe clean.

- Clean tile floors with ½ cup ARM & HAMMER Baking Soda in a bucket of warm water. Mop and rinse clean.

- Clean vinyl upholstery, such as that on a recliner or kitchen chair, with a paste of ARM & HAMMER Baking Soda and water. Rub it on, allow to dry, then wipe off.

- To clean a glass vase or similar container, fill it three-quarters full with hot water, add a teaspoon of ARM & HAMMER Baking Soda, and shake. Let sit, then rinse.

Carpet Freshener

Basic Recipe

> 1 cup crushed, dried herbs (rosemary, southernwood, lavender, etc.)
> 1 teaspoon McCormick Ground Cloves
> 1 teaspoon McCormick Ground Cinnamon
> 1 teaspoon ARM & HAMMER Baking Soda

Combine ingredients and sprinkle over carpet. Let sit for a few minutes, then vacuum.

Variations

Mix 1 small box ARM & HAMMER Baking Soda with a few drops of your favorite essential oil and sprinkle mixture onto carpet. Let sit 10 to 20 minutes, then vacuum.

Combine 1 cup ARM & HAMMER Baking Soda, 1 cup Argo Corn Starch, and 15 drops of your favorite essential oil. Leave on carpet 10 to 20 minutes, then vacuum. Store mixture in a glass jar or other airtight container.

- A fresh grease stain on a cloth chair can be absorbed with equal parts ARM & HAMMER Baking Soda and Morton Salt. Sprinkle the mixture onto the stain and rub lightly; leave on for a few hours, then vacuum.

- To remove silver tarnish, boil water and ½ teaspoon Morton Salt with 1 to 2 teaspoons ARM & HAMMER Baking Soda. Place tarnished silverware in a pan with the boiled mixture and a piece of Reynolds Wrap Aluminum Foil. Simmer for 2 to 3 minutes. Rinse the silverware well, then use a soft cloth to buff dry.

WHAT'S THAT SMELL?

- Add ARM & HAMMER Baking Soda to a vacuum bag to fight smells that can accumulate there.

- Before storing a piece of luggage, place an open box of ARM & HAMMER Baking Soda inside and close the luggage overnight. Repeat this when removing luggage from long-term storage.

- Eliminate residue and smells from mops or rags by soaking them in a mixture of 4 tablespoons ARM & HAMMER Baking Soda and 1 gallon water.

- Fill the toes of an old pair of pantyhose with ARM & HAMMER Baking Soda, cut off the feet, and tie to secure. Hang the sachets anywhere musty odors linger.

- Reduce garbage can smells by sprinkling ARM & HAMMER Baking Soda inside each time you add garbage.

 ◆ Control odor from a pet accident by leaving a thin layer of ARM & HAMMER Baking Soda on the affected area after cleaning. Vacuum when dry.

HOUSEFUL OF HINTS

Various Surfaces

◆ Candle wax can be removed from most hard surfaces with a paste of ARM & HAMMER Baking Soda and water. Scrub with a nylon scrubber.

◆ Clean chrome with a paste of ARM & HAMMER Baking Soda and water. Apply, then buff dry.

◆ Scour soot and ash from fireplace bricks with a solution of 4 tablespoons ARM & HAMMER Baking Soda and 1 quart warm water. Rub into bricks with a stiff brush.

Baby Business

◆ Sprinkle ARM & HAMMER Baking Soda on a damp O-Cel-O sponge to wipe down cribs, changing tables, baby mattresses, and playpens. Rinse areas thoroughly and allow to dry.

◆ To remove urine from a mattress, blot dry with Scott Towels or a rag, then sprinkle area with ARM & HAMMER Baking Soda. Let dry, then vacuum.

◆ Deodorize really smelly stuffed animals by placing them in a paper bag, adding ARM & HAMMER Baking Soda, and shaking vigorously. Store in bag overnight. If necessary, change the baking soda and repeat until odor is gone.

Cooking, Baking & Washing Up

Starting with the preparation of your ingredients and extending all the way through until the last pan is scrubbed, baking soda is a cook's best friend. All its gifts come into play—including texture, carbonation, and alkalinity. That's how it can clean, reduce acidity, tenderize, add fluffiness, increase digestibility, substitute for other ingredients, fix mistakes, and scrub pots and pans. ARM & HAMMER Baking Soda: not just for baking!

PREP WORK

Fruits and Veggies

◆ Sprinkle ARM & HAMMER Baking Soda on a damp O-Cel-O sponge and scrub your fruits and vegetables to remove dirt, wax, or pesticide residue. Rinse well.

◆ Sprinkle ARM & HAMMER Baking Soda on fresh pineapple to improve its flavor, especially if the pineapple is not quite ripe.

◆ Add a pinch of ARM & HAMMER Baking Soda to the water when soaking dried beans. It helps make them more digestible.

Surf and Turf

◆ Reduce that unpleasant fishy taste by soaking raw fish for at least half an hour in 2 tablespoons ARM &

HAMMER Baking Soda and 1 quart water. Rinse and cook.

◆ Tenderize tough meat by rubbing it with ARM & HAMMER Baking Soda. Let it stand for several hours, then rinse and cook.

◆ Rub ARM & HAMMER Baking Soda into the fat surrounding pork chops to make them crispier.

◆ Before cooking whole poultry, rinse in cold water and sprinkle ARM & HAMMER Baking Soda inside and out to tenderize. Refrigerate overnight. Rinse well.

CHEF'S HELPER
Cooking

◆ Add 1 teaspoon ARM & HAMMER Baking Soda to the water when cooking rice to improve fluffiness.

◆ Add a pinch of ARM & HAMMER Baking Soda to the water when boiling cabbage to tenderize and avoid overcooking.

◆ A pinch of ARM & HAMMER Baking Soda thrown into potatoes while mashing will make them fluffier.

Baking Soda at Its Best

◆ Test the freshness of ARM & HAMMER Baking Soda by pouring a small amount of Heinz Distilled White Vinegar or ReaLemon Lemon Juice over ½ teaspoon of baking soda. If it doesn't actively bubble, it's too old to use.

◆ A batter using ARM & HAMMER Baking Soda should be mixed and put in the oven quickly to retain the best leavening action.

- Eliminate the gaseous side effects of baked beans by adding a dash of ARM & HAMMER Baking Soda while cooking.

- Keep cauliflower white and its odor under control when boiling or steaming by adding 1 teaspoon ARM & HAMMER Baking Soda to the cooking water.

- When making fresh cranberry sauce, cover cranberries with water in a saucepan and bring to a boil. Add 1 tablespoon ARM & HAMMER Baking Soda, stir, drain, and return to heat. You'll need less sugar than usual to complete the sauce.

Baking

- When baking sour cream cake, combine the ARM & HAMMER Baking Soda and sour cream before mixing with other ingredients to activate the soda more quickly.

- To prevent cracks in homemade frosting, add a pinch of ARM & HAMMER Baking Soda before spreading it on a cake.

- Sweeten tart blackberries with ½ teaspoon ARM & HAMMER Baking Soda before adding any sugar when making pies or cobblers.

Substitutions

- Make self-rising flour with 3½ cups flour, 1¾ teaspoons Clabber Girl Baking Powder, 1¾ teaspoons ARM & HAMMER Baking Soda, and 1¾ teaspoons Morton Salt.

- Yeast can be replaced in a recipe with equal parts ARM & HAMMER Baking Soda and powdered vitamin C. The dough will rise during baking.

- Substitute 1 teaspoon ARM & HAMMER Baking Soda and 2 teaspoons Heinz Distilled White Vinegar for 2 eggs in any fruitcake or ginger cake recipe.

- In a recipe calling for sour milk or buttermilk, substitute fresh milk, adding ¾ teaspoon ARM & HAMMER Baking Soda to each cup needed.

Recipe Enhancements

- Adding 1 teaspoon ARM & HAMMER Baking Soda to the other dry ingredients in a chocolate cake will give the cake a darker color.

- Omelets get fluffier if you add ½ teaspoon ARM & HAMMER Baking Soda for every 3 eggs.

- When making fruitcake, add a teaspoon of ARM & HAMMER Baking Soda to darken the cake and soften the fruit a bit.

- Neutralize the acids in any recipe with a large amount of fruit by adding just a pinch of ARM & HAMMER Baking Soda.

- Add a pinch of ARM & HAMMER Baking Soda to a buttermilk waffle recipe to make the waffles lighter and softer.

- Cut the acidity of tomato sauce or chili by adding a pinch of ARM & HAMMER Baking Soda.

Problem Solving and Problem Prevention

- If you add too much vinegar to a recipe, add a pinch of ARM & HAMMER Baking Soda to counteract it.

- When gravy separates, a pinch of ARM & HAMMER Baking Soda may get oils and fats to stick back together.

- To test the acidity of canned tomatoes, dip a moist teaspoon in ARM & HAMMER Baking Soda and use it to stir the tomatoes. Bubbling means the acid level is high.

- Home-canned tomato juice may become too acidic. Add a bit of ARM & HAMMER Baking Soda before using it in cooking to cut the acidity.

- Anytime you might have to boil water before drinking it, soften it with 1 tablespoon ARM & HAMMER Baking Soda per gallon of water.

- Add a pinch of ARM & HAMMER Baking Soda to a cup of coffee to reduce its acidity.

- Add ¼ teaspoon ARM & HAMMER Baking Soda to 8 ounces of orange juice, grapefruit juice, or lemonade. This will add fizz to the drink and reduce its acidity.

DYNAMICS OF DISHWASHING

The Basics

- Clean silverware easily: Sprinkle some ARM & HAMMER Baking Soda on a damp cloth or an O-Cel-O sponge; rub silverware, rinse, and let dry.

- To freshen baby bottles, fill them with warm water and 1 teaspoon ARM & HAMMER Baking Soda. Shake and rinse, then clean as usual.

- Renew old sponges, nylon scrubbers, and scrub brushes—even bottle nipples and bottle brushes—by soaking them overnight in a solution of 4 tablespoons ARM & HAMMER Baking Soda to 1 quart water.

Stubborn Stuff

- A paste of ARM & HAMMER Baking Soda and water removes stains from plastic and rubber utensils. Apply with an O-Cel-O sponge.

- Scrub stained plastic storage containers with a paste of ReaLemon Lemon Juice and ARM & HAMMER Baking Soda.

- Clean the oil out of a salad dressing cruet by shaking ARM & HAMMER Baking Soda inside, then rinsing it clean with warm water.

- Deodorize and remove stains from wooden bowls or utensils with a solution of 4 tablespoons ARM & HAMMER Baking Soda to 1 quart water.

- To clean a teapot or stovetop per-colator, fill it with water, add 2 or 3 tablespoons ARM & HAMMER Baking Soda, and boil for 10 to 15 minutes. After cooling, scrub and rinse thoroughly.

- Dip a damp O-Cel-O sponge in ARM & HAMMER Baking Soda and rub coffee mug and teacup stains away. Particularly stubborn stains may also require a little Morton Salt.

Pots & Pans & Such

◆ Clean encrusted grease and food on roasting pans by dampening with hot water and sprinkling on ARM & HAMMER Baking Soda. Let sit for an hour and sponge clean.

◆ To loosen baked- or dried-on food from a pan, gently boil water and ARM & HAMMER Baking Soda in the pan. When food is loosened, allow pan to cool and then wipe clean.

◆ Enamel cookware can't handle abrasive cleaners. Instead, apply a paste of ARM & HAMMER Baking Soda and water and let sit for an hour. Clean with an O-Cel-O No-Scratch Scrub Sponge and rinse.

◆ Sprinkle ARM & HAMMER Baking Soda over burned-on stains on cookie sheets, then cover with hot water. Let soak for 10 minutes. Next, scour with baking soda and an O-Cel-O No-Scratch Scrub Sponge.

◆ Loosen burned-on food from a barbecue grill rack by first enclosing it in a large plastic bag; combine 1 cup ARM & HAMMER Baking Soda and ½ cup Parsons' Ammonia and pour mixture in bag over rack. Close the bag and let rack sit overnight. Scrub and rinse well in the morning. Be sure to wear rubber gloves and work in a well-ventilated area.

Laundry and Clothing Care

Tough and tender: a perfect description of ARM & HAMMER Baking Soda and exactly the qualities you need for the challenges of washday and wardrobe. Baking soda works to freshen, clean, and remove odors, with enough power left over to help other laundry and clothing care products do their jobs. Yet it's also safe for all the fabrics and folks in your household.

LAUNDRY DAY BASICS

◆ Add ½ cup ARM & HAMMER Baking Soda to your Tide laundry detergent to freshen laundry and help the detergent work harder.

◆ To brighten colored clothes that can't tolerate chlorine bleach, add ½ cup ARM & HAMMER Baking Soda to your wash along with your Tide laundry detergent. Then add ½ cup Heinz Distilled White Vinegar to the final rinse.

◆ Use ARM & HAMMER Baking Soda instead of fabric softener. Add ½ cup during the rinse cycle.

◆ Add ½ cup ARM & HAMMER Baking Soda (only ¼ cup for front-loading machines) with the usual amount of Clorox Regular-Bleach to increase whitening power.

THE NOSE KNOWS

◆ Freshen laundry hampers by sprinkling ARM & HAMMER Baking Soda over dirty clothes as they await washing.

◆ Remove the smell of cigarette smoke in clothes by soaking them in a solution of 4 tablespoons ARM & HAMMER Baking Soda to 1 quart water before washing.

◆ If your baby spits up on his shirt or yours, moisten a cloth, dip it in ARM & HAMMER Baking Soda, and dab at the spot. The odor will be controlled until the clothing can be changed.

STAIN, BE GONE!

◆ For perspiration stains, scrub in a paste of ARM & HAMMER Baking Soda and water; let sit for 1 hour, then launder.

Pretreating Stains

Make your own pretreating stain remover. Mix together ¼ cup Parsons' Ammonia, ¼ cup Heinz Distilled White Vinegar, ⅛ cup ARM & HAMMER Baking Soda, 1 tablespoon Ivory Liquid Hand Cleanser, and 1 quart water. Pour mixture into a labeled spray bottle. Apply solution to stains, let sit for a few minutes, then launder as usual. A variation: Use soap flakes and ARM & HAMMER Baking Soda when washing stained natural fabrics. Add 1 tablespoon Heinz Distilled White Vinegar to the rinse cycle to keep colors bright.

- To remove a bloodstain, dampen the area with water and rub with ARM & HAMMER Baking Soda. Follow by dabbing with Rite Aid hydrogen peroxide until the stain is gone. Test for colorfastness first.

- If you have stained your white clothes by washing them with colored ones, undo the damage by soaking them in warm water to which you have added ARM & HAMMER Baking Soda, Morton Salt, and Tide laundry detergent.

- An ink stain on leather can be removed by laying the item flat and sprinkling ARM & HAMMER Baking Soda on the stain. Leave on until ink is absorbed, brush off, and repeat if necessary.

SPECIAL LAUNDRY CHALLENGES

- Rinse pool chlorine out of bathing suits in a sink full of water with 1 tablespoon ARM & HAMMER Baking Soda added.

- Even if a tag says "dry-clean only," some items can be cleaned with a solution of 4 tablespoons ARM & HAMMER Baking Soda in a sink of cold water. Test for colorfastness first.

- Brighten yellowed linens by adding 4 tablespoons ARM & HAMMER Baking Soda to the wash water.

- If you've washed a crayon with a load of clothes, rewash the load with the hottest possible water, adding a half to a full box of ARM & HAMMER Baking Soda. Repeat if necessary.

- Clean suede with ARM & HAMMER Baking Soda applied with a soft brush. Let it sit, then brush it off.

CARING FOR BABY CLOTHES

- Add ½ cup ARM & HAMMER Baking Soda to Tide powdered or liquid laundry detergent to freshen clothes and help improve the detergent's performance on baby food stains. If using powdered laundry detergent, add baking soda in the rinse cycle only.

- Before putting new baby clothes on your child, remove chemical finishes from the clothes by washing them in mild soap and ½ cup ARM & HAMMER Baking Soda.

FOOTNOTES ON SOCKS AND SHOES

- Keep smelly feet at bay by sprinkling ARM & HAMMER Baking Soda into socks and shoes before wearing to control odor and moisture.

- Clean the rubber on athletic shoes with ARM & HAMMER Baking Soda sprinkled on an O-Cel-O sponge or a washcloth.

- Before applying shoe polish, remove black scuff marks with a paste of ARM & HAMMER Baking Soda and water.

Household Projects and Maintenance

Taking care of the homestead is a big responsibility. Baking soda to the rescue! Keeping your car looking sharp, tending a garden or a household plant, battling as a weekend warrior—it can all be overwhelming. But you know where to turn: Go to the kitchen. There's a box of ARM & HAMMER Baking Soda with your name on it. (Even if you don't actually answer to "ARM & HAMMER.")

FIRE FACTS

Note: Call 911 if you think a fire is out of hand. Once a cooking fire is extinguished, allow pots and their contents to cool before removing pots from the stove for cleaning.

◆ Keep a box of ARM & HAMMER Baking Soda within reach of the stove (but far enough away to be out of range of a fire). Pour baking soda directly on the flames to extinguish a small fire.

◆ Do not use ARM & HAMMER Baking Soda to extinguish a fire in a deep-fat fryer; the hot fat may splatter.

◆ Keep a spray bottle of 1 teaspoon ARM & HAMMER Baking Soda mixed with 1 pint of water by your grill. If grease drips onto coals during grilling, control any flames by lightly spraying mixture onto coals.

- Do not use ARM & HAMMER Baking Soda on any fire involving combustibles, such as wood or paper.

HANDYPERSON HINTS

- A permanent filler for nail holes in white walls is a paste of ARM & HAMMER Baking Soda and Elmer's Glue-All.

- You can fill a crack or small gap in wood, metal, or plastic by sprinkling ARM & HAMMER Baking Soda into the opening and then dripping Instant Krazy Glue over it until the gap is filled.

- Revive hardened paintbrush bristles by boiling them in ½ gallon water, 1 cup ARM & HAMMER Baking Soda, and ¼ cup Heinz Distilled White Vinegar.

Chemistry Class

- *Baking soda* is the common term for *bicarbonate of soda,* which in turn is more formally called either *sodium bicarbonate* or *sodium hydrogen carbonate.* It results when sodium carbonate (soda ash) is treated with carbon dioxide. But what's in a name?

- Baking powder is produced from an alkali-acid combination—specifically, baking soda and cream of tartar (tartaric acid).

- Because it's a source of carbon dioxide, sodium bicarbonate is used in effervescent salts, carbonated beverages, tanning leather, wool preparation, and dry-chemical fire extinguishers. When the extinguisher is turned upside down, sodium bicarbonate mixes and reacts with sulfuric acid to propel water.

OUTDOOR CHORES

- Dip a damp wire brush into ARM & HAMMER Baking Soda and use it to clean door and window screens. Scrub, then rinse screens with an O-Cel-O sponge or a hose.

- Clean lawn furniture at the start of the season with a solution of ¼ cup ARM & HAMMER Baking Soda in 1 quart warm water. Wipe and rinse.

- Absorb an oily stain on deck wood by sprinkling the affected area with ARM & HAMMER Baking Soda and letting it sit for 1 hour. Repeat if necessary.

- Clean a cement birdbath by sprinkling it with ARM & HAMMER Baking Soda. Scrub and rinse.

- Control odors in your compost pile by sprinkling it every now and then with ARM & HAMMER Baking Soda.

CAR CARE AND GARAGE GRUNGE

- Use ARM & HAMMER Baking Soda to safely clean your car's lights, chrome, windows, tires, vinyl seats, floor mats, and wiper blades. Sprinkle it onto a damp O-Cel-O sponge, scrub, and rinse.

- To remove car odors, simply sprinkle ARM & HAMMER Baking Soda on the seats and carpets. Let it sit at least half an hour, then vacuum.

- Clean up spots on upholstery by rubbing in a paste of ARM & HAMMER Baking Soda and water. Let dry, then vacuum.

- Sprinkle equal parts ARM & HAMMER Baking Soda and Quaker Yellow Corn Meal on light oil spills in the garage. Let dry, then sweep or vacuum away.

USE YOUR GREEN THUMB

- To test the acidity of your garden soil, add a pinch of ARM & HAMMER Baking Soda to 1 tablespoon of soil. If it fizzes, the soil's pH level is probably less than 5.0.

- Geraniums, begonias, hydrangeas, and other flowers that prefer alkaline soil should be watered occasionally with a solution of 3 tablespoons ARM & HAMMER Baking Soda to 1 quart water.

- Carnations, mums, and petunias prefer neutral soil. To raise potting soil alkalinity, apply a solution of 4 table-spoons ARM & HAMMER Baking Soda to 1 quart water. Use sparingly.

- Sprinkle ARM & HAMMER Baking Soda lightly around tomato plants. This will sweeten the tomatoes by lowering soil acidity.

- Before placing them in a vase, briefly dip the stems of cut flowers in a solution of 4 tablespoons ARM & HAMMER Baking Soda and 1 quart water to lengthen their life.

Homemade Plant Food

1 teaspoon Clabber Girl Baking Powder
½ teaspoon Parsons' Ammonia
1 tablespoon Rite Aid Epsom salts
1 teaspoon Morton Salt
1 gallon water

Mix ingredients together and store in a spray bottle. Shake well before using. Spray household plants once a month.

Arts & Crafts, Pets & Pastimes

In this section, we'll discover the lighter side of ARM & HAMMER Baking Soda. Kids of all ages can enjoy holiday and everyday crafts. Pets and their owners can learn to face scary words such as *bath* and *litter box.* It's remarkable what a small box of white crystals can accomplish.

HOLIDAYS AND EVERY DAY

♦ Here's an idea for an unusual centerpiece: Fill a vase with water, add a few drops of McCormick Food Color and ¼ cup Heinz Distilled White Vinegar, and then pour in 3 teaspoons ARM & HAMMER Baking Soda. Drop in buttons, rice, or pasta and watch them rise and fall like magic.

♦ Use ARM & HAMMER Baking Soda to simulate snow on your Christmas tree.

THOSE WONDERFUL PETS
Staying Healthy

♦ To deodorize your pet's bedding, sprinkle the area with ARM & HAMMER Baking Soda, let stand 15 minutes, and vacuum.

♦ If your pet has a run-in with a skunk, wash the pet in a bath containing 1 quart Rite Aid hydrogen peroxide,

¼ cup ARM & HAMMER Baking Soda, and 1 teaspoon Ivory Liquid Hand Cleanser. Rinse well and dry. Discard unused cleaner.

◆ After making sure the stinger is removed, cover a bee sting on your pet with a paste of ARM & HAMMER Baking Soda and water.

Good Grooming

◆ Give your dog or cat a dry bath by sprinkling it with ARM & HAMMER Baking Soda. Rub in, then brush out.

◆ For a wet wash, combine 3 tablespoons ARM & HAMMER Baking Soda with 1 teaspoon Dawn dishwashing liquid and 1 teaspoon Johnson's Baby Oil in a spray bottle. Fill bottle with water and spritz your pet, working solution into the hair and skin. Rinse and wipe dry.

◆ Gently brush your pet's teeth with a damp, soft Reach toothbrush dipped in ARM & HAMMER Baking Soda.

Cleaning Up

◆ To eliminate odors from litter boxes, sprinkle in ½ cup ARM & HAMMER Baking Soda.

◆ Clean the kitty litter pan by removing litter and pouring in ½ inch Heinz Distilled White Vinegar. Let stand, then pour out and dry. Sprinkle ARM & HAMMER Baking Soda over the bottom before adding fresh kitty litter.

◆ Make your own natural litter by mixing a small box of ARM & HAMMER Baking Soda with 2 to 3 inches of dry, sandy clay.

Trademark Information

Argo Corn Starch® is a registered trademark of the ACH Food Companies, Inc.

ARM & HAMMER® is a registered trademark of Church & Dwight Co., Inc.

Clabber Girl Baking Powder® is a registered trademark of Clabber Girl Corporation.

Clorox® is a registered trademark of The Clorox Company.

Crest® is a registered trademark of Procter & Gamble.

Dawn® is a registered trademark of Procter & Gamble.

Domino Sugar® is a registered trademark of Domino Foods, Inc.

Elmer's® is a registered trademark of Borden.

GLAD® is a registered trademark of Union Carbide Corporation.

Heinz® is a registered trademark of H. J. Heinz Company.

Ivory® is a registered trademark of Procter & Gamble.

Johnson's® is a registered trademark of Johnson & Johnson.

McCormick® is a registered trademark of McCormick & Company, Incorporated.

Morton Salt® is a registered trademark of Morton International, Inc.

O-Cel-O® is a registered trademark of 3M.

Parsons'® is a registered trademark of Church & Dwight Co., Inc.

Quaker® is a registered trademark of the Quaker Oats Company.

Reach® is a registered trademark of Johnson & Johnson.

ReaLemon® is a registered trademark of Borden.

ReaLime® is a registered trademark of Borden.

Reynolds Wrap® is a registered trademark of Reynolds Metals.

Rite Aid® is a registered trademark of the Rite Aid Corporation.

Scott Towels® is a registered trademark of Kimberly-Clark Worldwide, Inc.

Tide® is a registered trademark of Procter & Gamble.

20 Mule Team Borax® is a registered trademark of The Dial Corporation.